# ANNA BARRIBALL

# CONTENTS

4

PREFACE

FIONA BRADLEY / ANTHONY SPIRA

25

FINDING A WAY THROUGH

FIONA BRADLEY

52

WATCH IT CLOSELY

BRIONY FER

88

IN CONVERSATION

ANNA BARRIBALL / ANTHONY SPIRA

104

PLATE LIST

106

BIOGRAPHY / BIBLIOGRAPHY

110

ACKNOWLEDGEMENTS

# PREFACE

FIONA BRADLEY / ANTHONY SPIRA

Anna Barriball makes work which moves between drawing and sculpture, often using the practice of drawing to create something which might be more properly understood to be sculpture. Sheets of paper pressed insistently by her pencil up against windows, walls and doors become heavily material objects, while things in the world – windbreaks, found photographs, a fireplace – are redrawn as artworks through subtle alteration.

This book is published by The Fruitmarket Gallery and MK Gallery on the occasion of two exhibitions of the work of Anna Barriball, and looks back over her practice since 2000, giving an insight into the development of her artistic language. We are pleased and proud to present this thoughtful, beautiful work in our galleries, and to extend the reach of both exhibitions with this publication.

We are grateful to a number of individuals and organisations who have helped with the exhibitions and publication, both financially and with their time and expertise. The exhibition is supported by The Henry Moore Foundation, who do so much for sculpture and for the organisations that show it. We thank them, and also the Exhibition Circle of Friends of MK Gallery and the Commissioning Patrons of The Fruitmarket Gallery. In preparing the exhibition, we are indebted to lenders, both public and private, who have generously agreed to be parted from works in their collection; and to Frith Street Gallery, London, who represent the artist, and whose financial investment has made this book possible.

The book has been created in close collaboration with Anna Barriball. As well as images of existing work, it includes images of new work, photographed in Milton Keynes just as the book was going to press. We are grateful to Gautier Deblonde for his wonderful photographs. We are pleased to publish a new essay by Briony Fer, who writes of drawing and drawing breath, of the dilemmas of looking, and of lightness and slightness as keys to the power of Barriball's work. We have both enjoyed thinking, speaking and writing about the work during the last year, and are pleased to have the opportunity to publish a conversation with the artist which was recorded during the preparation of the exhibition in Milton Keynes.

Final thanks, of course, go to Anna Barriball. For giving so unstintingly of her time, energy and ideas, and for her work.

Fiona Bradley
Director, The Fruitmarket Gallery, Edinburgh

Anthony Spira
Director, MK Gallery, Milton Keynes

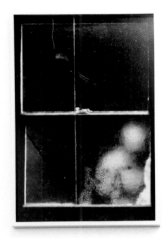

*Untitled*, 2011, marker pen on windbreaks, metal poles

8   *Untitled*, 2011 (detail)

10    *Untitled*, 2011 (detail)

*Untitled III*, 2008, ink on paper

*Untitled VII*, *Untitled V*, *Untitled XII*, 2004, ink and bubble mixture on found photographs    13

*Copper Pipes*, 2011, acrylic paint on paper

*Untitled II*, 2008, ink on paper; *Yellow Leaves*, 2011, curtain fabric    15

*Yellow Leaves*, 2011, curtain fabric

*Window*, 2002, pencil on paper

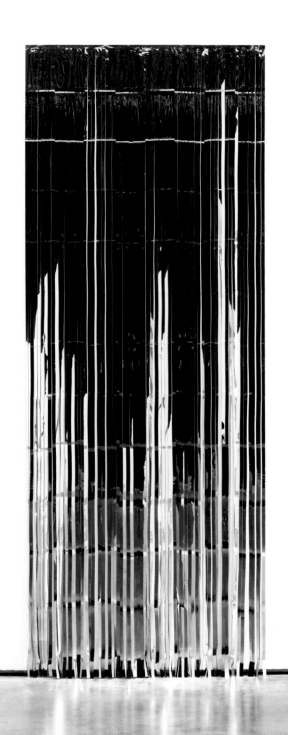

*Shutters*, 2011, diptych, pencil on paper

# FINDING A WAY THROUGH
## FIONA BRADLEY

'For you know what they say…
If the wolves come out of the walls,
Then it's all over.'[1]

Anna Barriball's *One Square Foot V* (2001, pp.28–29)
is a drawing (one foot square) of one square foot of
wooden floorboards. It is a drawing of floorboards made
by drawing on the floorboards; putting a piece of paper
down on the floor and drawing. Drawing in an abstract
way, with a repetitive sequence of straight lines which
have nothing and everything to do with describing the
floorboards beneath. The drawing is the floorboards, the
floorboards are the drawing – there's a claustrophobically
tight circularity between medium and message going
on here.

In conversation about her practice, Barriball has spoken
of finding 'ways through'. Yet in this drawing, and in
many of her others, it takes a while to understand the
relevance of this comment. *One Square Foot V* seems
precisely not about finding a way through – like *Brick
Wall* (2005, p.35), *Door* (2004, pp.19, 38) and *Shutters*
(2011, pp.22–24), the surface of this image *is* the image,
it pulls you up short in contemplation of the thingness
of the thing it is. And there is something ominous about
that. The process at work in these works is not one

which invites fantastical vision on the part of the artist
or imaginative speculation on the part of the viewer
(what we see is what we see and the meaning of the
works seem nothing more or less than the fact of their
existence). Yet there is something about their blunt
insistence on being exactly what they are that leads
to the sense that there may be something more – they
may be blocking something off, or something in.

A drawing that shares a process with these four works
is not, however, quite so insistently what it seems,
or rather hints at being rather more than it at first
seems. *Untitled* (2009, p.43) describes in pencil a section
of brick wall. Yet closer inspection reveals the drawing to
have taken its image from a bricked-up door. If we look
carefully, we can see an alteration in the pattern of bricks
over the door's lintel, and a shift in the bricks' regularity
where the bricked-up void meets the original wall. This
must be why the proportions of the drawing are that of
a door, and why the way the frame frames the drawing
suggests the frame of a door. But maybe, also, we read
the drawing as being of a door because we want it to
suggest a way through – we want to think that there is
or was in fact something behind the bricks; that there
is an implied depth to the drawing, even though we
know, because we understand the process by which it
was made, that there cannot be. Maybe we need to insert

an imagined narrative that this is a door that has been bricked-up for a purpose in order to articulate the vague sense of there being a reason for the drawing's material muteness, that like the previous drawings it might in fact be hiding something behind its formal declaration that what we see is all there is. But, of course, what we see *is* all there is – the drawing might toy with the narrative potential of the idea of a bricked-up door but is actually only really a section of brick wall drawn just like *Brick Wall*, the pencil transcribing the exact image of the bricks beneath the paper.

There is something in our (and presumably the artist's) desire for a way through, though, that haunts the work. Barriball returns again and again to doors and windows, subjects that by their very nature offer precisely that. Once a window has been drawn over repeatedly with graphite, as in *Window* (2002, p.20) and a series of drawings of art deco windows called *Sunrise/Sunset* (2008, 2010, pp.98–99) it becomes its very antithesis. Barriball's windows are opaque, leaden, the paper buckled, made heavy with pencil, scarred by the forms it describes, marked by the time it has taken to describe them. More sculptures than drawings, they take on the form of their subjects while denying the very things that make them what they are. Treated in this way, they are more wall than window, their materiality throwing us back into the room with them, rather than inviting us through.

Another series of works called *Mirror Window Wall* (2008, pp.32–33) shows that Barriball has, of course, thought this through. A mirror is a silvered window. A wall is one bricked-up. The works are all three. In each, four sections of brick wall are first silvered with ink to look almost like mirrors, then hung four square to look almost like the panes of a window, the gap between them mimicking a window frame. The work plays with positive and negative, opaque and transparent, inviting us through only to rebuff us over and over again – physically, conceptually, linguistically. These works are de-natured objects. They perhaps belong in the register of the Freudian uncanny – things which we think we know, but in fact do not. They certainly allude to it.

*Untitled II* and *III* (2008, pp.12, 15) are weighty, sculptural forms which lean into corners. Reminiscent of buckled sheet metal, they are in fact ink on paper;

drawings given shape this time not by the memory of a form beneath but one within (we learn from Briony Fer's essay in this publication that, to make the works, Barriball first covered a large sheet of paper in ink, then wrapped it round herself). Uncanny again, these works are the gestures of drawing writ large, made into sculpture twice over. There is a whiff of art history about them both as performance and as sculpture – they speak of Yves Klein painting with bodies, of Richard Serra folding and pouring metal, of Eva Hesse making sculptures, often out of similarly two-dimensional materials which speak eloquently of the actions by which they were brought into being. Again, like the windows, their insistent materiality keeps the viewer very definitely alongside them in the space they occupy.

These works have recently been joined by a new set of rolled paper sculptures, *Copper Pipes* (2011, p.14) – paper painted with copper-coloured acrylic paint. These, more immaculate than *Untitled II* and *III*, mimic the form of copper plumbing tubes. Beautiful in their metallic, shimmering sheen, they seem to be testing out what paper can do, how much form it can take on. As sculptures, they are material action – paper drawn on, rolled up, propped up.

These works are de-natured paper; paper made solid and self-supporting. The register of the uncanny is evoked not so much in the order of representation (I don't think it worries us unduly if copper pipes turn out to be not quite what they seem), but in the medium in which they are made. These are drawings which have transformed their support not only in the way they look (we expect, in fact demand this of art) but in how they behave.

And maybe there is a destructive impulse at work here – as if the marks covering the paper, transforming it from one kind of thing to another, are as much about defacing it as they are embellishing. Maybe we are in the realm of the kind of transgression beloved by Georges Bataille, of the *informe* or formless, of drawing understood as a primal urge to deface the pure whiteness and paperiness of paper. This idea seems to work with *One Square Foot V*, *Brick Wall*, *Door* and *Shutters*, the drawings with which I started, in which paper is forced by a pencil to bend to the will of a shape behind it. There are also other works of Barriball's in which this kind of idea comes to the fore. The early *Black*

*Wardrobe* (2003, p.31), a wardrobe wrapped in tape, has been discussed in terms of the Freudian uncanny. Yet it might also partake of the Bataillian formless, the tape rendering the wardrobe useless, functionless, turning it away from what it was meant to be, bringing down (to use a Bataillian phrase) its meaning and function in the world. A collection of found slides has been rendered similarly useless in *Untitled (80 slides)* (2005, p.71). Leaving the set of slides as she found them in a market, wrapped in tape, Barriball ensures the images they contain are forever inaccessible. In a related work of 2006, *Untitled I–V*, the projection of a different set of slides revels in the unconscious beauty of destruction and loss (pp.66–69). These slides are on the brink of extinction, their images so badly deteriorated as to be almost illegible. Photographed and re-projected in Barriball's work, the areas of damage which encroach on the slides' original imagery are in themselves very beautiful, but are about loss first and foremost.

In *Knife II* (2004, p.30) Barriball plays again with the idea of the destruction of the surface, and with making paper behave in a way we might not expect it to. To make it, she drew round the blade of a knife and then sewed with black thread over and under the image. Stabbing up and down through the paper, her process results in the 'blade' of the knife being pulled forward, completely wrapped in black thread. The blackness of the knife is a shock against the whiteness of the paper, and its solidity and three-dimensionality a contrast to the paper's smooth surface. The work speaks of the actions of its making – stabbing, puncturing, defiling, but also wrapping and repairing.

Maybe it is action, the way that her drawings and sculptures are materialised action, that gives us a clue to how Barriball understands the idea of finding a way through. Maybe it is not the way through an image she is after, but a way through *to* an image – a way of making an image out of an idea or an object or a material. For a new work, she takes cheap plastic windbreaks and colours them in, disfiguring with black marker pen the iconic blue, yellow and red of the British seaside staple (pp.6–11). Denied their colour, the windbreaks are then denied their function, hung against a wall so that they stand no chance of rebuffing a wind. By making them what they are not, Barriball

somehow insists on what they are, and we seem to be back to that idea of the thingness of the thing that marked *One Square Foot V*. And also the sense of the ominous that came with it. Though here, that which was underplayed in *One Square Foot V* is played out. The windbreak work is not placed exactly against the wall – there is a gap behind it. From this gap, the stripes of colour in the windbreaks, the colour that has been suffocated by the artist's marker pen, glows brightly. It is as though the windbreaks do after all offer a way through, that there is space behind them, possibly some kind of transcendental space. Still, it does not welcome us through – it keeps us where we are, wondering about it.

*The Way We Should Have Gone* (2010, p.81), a work which takes the form of a poster for an exhibition that never happened, is a picture of a way through – a winding path in a leafless, wintry wood. A classic trope of memory, misunderstanding and discovery, particularly with reference to the self (think of the path in the wood on which Dante finds himself at the beginning of his *Inferno*), the woodland path in this work opens Barriball's practice to the space of myth. Myths, to quote A.S. Byatt, 'are often unsatisfactory, even tormenting. They puzzle and haunt the mind that encounters them. They shape different parts of the world inside our heads, and they shape them not as pleasures, but as encounters with the inapprehensible'.[2] The way we should have gone, the path we might have taken, the story that could have been told – art, in the mythic sense, as a way to describe something we don't understand and don't yet know the answer to. Art as a way, possibly, to acknowledge the wolves in the walls while finding a way to keep them there where they belong.

References

1. Neil Gaiman, *The Wolves in the Walls*, Bloomsbury, London 2003, unpaginated

2. A.S. Byatt, 'Thoughts on Myths', in A.S. Byatt, *Ragnarok: The End of the Gods*, Canongate, Edinburgh, 2011, p.161

*One Square Foot V*, 2001, pencil on paper

*Knife II*, 2004, cotton and paper

*Mirror Window Wall I*, 2008, ink on paper    33

*Brick Wall*, 2005, pencil on paper   35

*Wall Mirrors*, 2007, diptych, silver pencil on paper

38    *Door*, 2004, pencil on paper

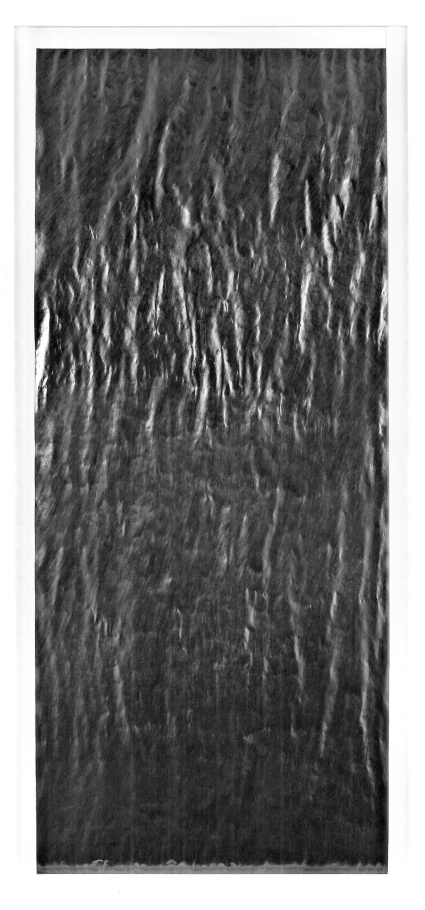

*Untitled*, 2007, pencil on paper   39

*Untitled (front door)*, 2007, pencil on paper

*Untitled (back door)*, 2006, pencil on paper   41

*Green Glass*, 2008, ink on paper

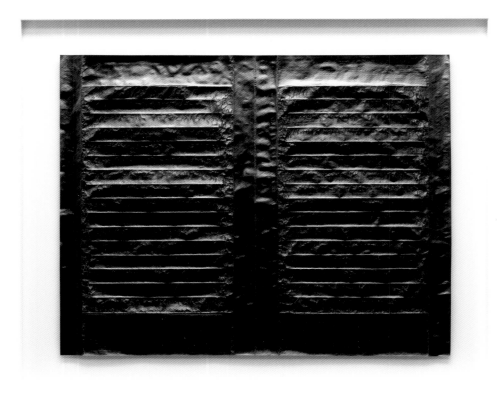

*Shutters with Fire Red*, 2011, pencil, paper, acrylic spray paint on board

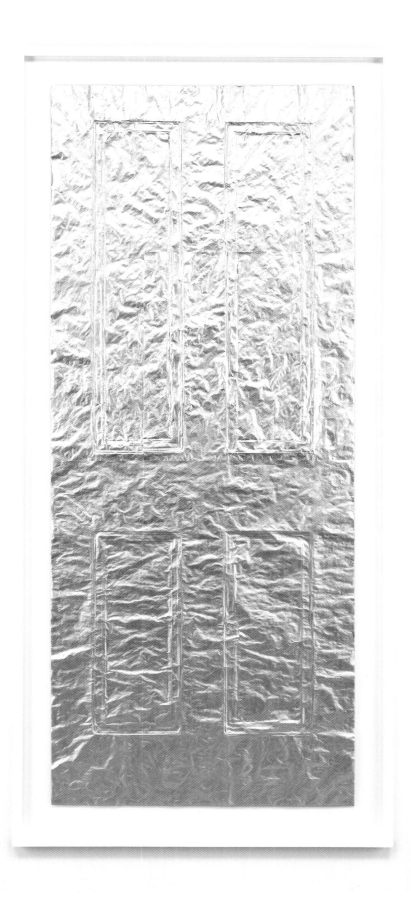

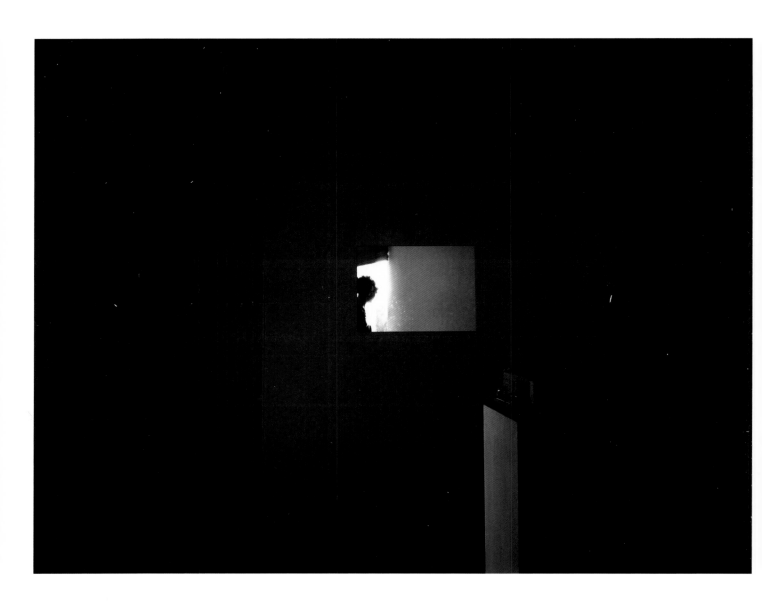

*Projection*, 2003, video projection

# WATCH IT CLOSELY

## BRIONY FER

On occasions, Anna Barriball makes work that is almost not there at all. Even though the making of the work may be quite laborious, even though it might be a very material thing that is made, it can end up hovering almost beneath the threshold of the visible. The work has about it a quiet agitation – and it quite often agitates at the edges of the field of vision. The words that come to mind for these kinds of effects are words like modest, understated, precarious, fleeting, fugitive – all of which have a bearing on the work, but are also not quite adequate to it. Agitation may be quiet but it can also contradict and transform what you think you know and what you feel about things. Over time, and this is the *work* of the work that really takes time, it comes to seem more and more resilient. It is as if the slighter it feels – the nearer nothing – the stronger and more demanding of our attention it is.

In 2005, Barriball made a short film that she called *Draw (fireplace)*, which runs to 10½ minutes. It consists of a single image of a sheet of tracing paper placed over an empty grate. As we watch, the paper 'breathes' in and out, very gently. The air is sucked in one moment pressing hard against the shape beneath, moulding to it, then billows out a little as the air blows out – or so it seems. Through the tracing paper you can just about see the patterns on the tiles underneath. Of course it is

mesmerising even though nothing happens except these small movements. It looks like the way a sheet of newspaper is placed over a fireplace to make a fire draw – except here there are no hands to hold it in place – as if the screen is its own giant lung. In fact it was made by opening and closing a door, creating a similar effect to one she had previously observed on a windy day. At the end of the film there is a bang which marks the moment the door flew out of her hand. But none of this is visible, so what is left is a simple repetitive action which actually 'aerates' the space of the film.

The word 'draw', in Barriball's work, can never be far away from the activity of drawing, which is what she does a lot of the time. But, in turn, drawing as a way of making things is intimately connected with the bodily action of breathing and the bodily product that is breath. Following this thread, it is not hard to see *Draw (fireplace)* coming out of her practice of drawing. In a 2002 work called *36 Breaths* (pp.60–61) for example, she collected into a grid 36 found photographs of a family on holiday. Over each of them she deposited a drop of Indian ink and then blew on it to make it spread out in small and spidery black tentacles. The pictures are small, from another time, images of familiar and familial behaviour – walking along a promenade in some seaside place, posing slightly stiffly in groups,

staring out into some unknown future, like anybody's relatives. The black blots spoil the photos and hide their contents but themselves look like very delicate specimens, ink rather than insect specimens.

Why do the people in found photographs look so lost? Because they are lost to us, I suppose. There is something odd about their distance from us, yet the implied intimacy with which we peer at them, into them even. The question ends up being not about why people look lost in old photos, but why do we, as viewing subjects, get lost in them; and not only in photos but in all art where the stakes are high enough for us to be worth losing ourselves.

In 2004, Barriball made another series using found photographs, *Untitled I–XII* (pp.13, 62–65). The photographs are black and white and sometimes creased, and those aspects are just as intimate and affective as the strangers that fill the frame – often young people, often but not always from the 1960s, often on holiday. This time she blew bubbles with a detergent mixed with ink onto the surfaces of the photos. When the bubble burst it left its liquid traces, the perfect circumference containing delicate swirls. The action doesn't amount to much, but the result is to open the photograph to something that it isn't. A different kind of space for sure, but also a different kind of time, as if a bubble – so transitory and impermanent – is some kind of air pocket for time past that is quite as powerful as the photo. The residue of the bubble mixture creates a kind of Proustian lens – a temporal lens that is strange yet familiar, found only to be lost.

Maybe these are not just photographs but a way of drawing breath, that is, drawings *of* breath. The minimal interaction that is blowing a bubble – so delicate, evanescent, momentary – leaves a deposit of automatic rivulets and blooms of liquefied movement. All because of a bit of air that was an exhaled breath. This is reminiscent of Piero Manzoni's dedication in the late 1950s to art that was pneumatic. In works such as *Artist's Breath* (1960) he blew up balloons and then, once they had lost the air they contained and had shrivelled, fixed them to a wooden plaque. This was part of Manzoni's conversation with Marcel Duchamp, who had posed the enigmatic question of 'draft pistons' in the erotic machinery of his famous work *The Bride Stripped*

*Bare By Her Bachelors, Even* (*The Large Glass*) (1915–23), but who has also named a photograph of a piece of net hung across a window *Current of Air*.

The residue or trace of the bubble mixture is not separate from the photograph, but instead causes the whole image to deliquesce. It hides the image but also ends up revealing another much stranger image in the process. When, a little later on, Barriball found some old 35mm slides that had deteriorated very badly, she said she saw what she had been trying to do in her previous series of found photographs. All she did with the slides was to re-photograph them in order to stabilise the images as they were – perilously close to a point of no return where they would have disappeared entirely. She then projected them onto a wall at a relatively small scale (pp.66–69). In what look like slides burnt by a projector, the dissolution of the image is almost total: a family group set against forest and mountains barely glimpsed between, or a ghostly figure in a bikini all but dissolved in psychedelic fronds of colour. One image is in the process of disappearing but it gives way – it yields – to another, whose medium is partly celluloid, partly time itself. The little stack of slide mounts, *Untitled (80 slides)* (2005, p.71) – where no images are visible at all – just completes this movement.

Barriball has said that she is interested in windows because they draw attention to the 'dilemmas of looking'. Windows of all shapes and sizes appear in her work. In 2006 she made a group of works using, again, found photographs, this time of buildings, where everything except a single small window was edited out with a sheet of white paper (*Windows 1–10*, pp.72–77). Removing everything like this is the reverse of collage. It leaves a single aperture marooned on an empty sheet, so a miniature window becomes a postage stamp-sized, inscrutable patch of dark. What you can't see is as important as what you can.

And then there are the rubbings that she has taken. In *Mirror Window Wall I* (2008, pp.32–33) the four 'panes' are each framed and arranged close together, leaving a narrow gap between them that mimics a cross bar in a window frame. The parts that stand in for the glass are impressions of a brick wall. And they shine, like a mirror. There is a whole dynamic of the look being blocked off rather than transparent – of being reflected back onto the viewer as a mirrored surface might. Rather than providing a transparent surface to look through, the dilemmas of looking take place in that space of the encounter – between the work and the viewer, not beyond it. It is not for nothing that bricked-up windows are called 'blind'. Or for that matter, that blinds are called 'blinds'.

As these life-size drawings have developed, they have become extremely diverse and varied. In 2000, shortly after leaving Chelsea College of Art, Barriball made a gold five pound note – by colouring it in with a gold pen (p.83). Looked at very closely, the image is all but concealed, leaving only an embossed texture and a remarkable miniature terrain of tiny creases and folds. *Silver Map* (2003, pp.86–87) works the same way – laid out flat and covered with silver pen it lays bare the folds and creases, as well as the incredibly faint but palpable ridges of a world map. The move to taking rubbings from existing surfaces comes a little bit later and continues to offer new possibilities. The spiralling coils of pencil sharpenings that lie everywhere around her studio bear witness to the laborious and time-consuming manner in which she makes these works. Even the smaller ones are incredibly labour intensive.

*Sunrise/Sunset* is a series of works begun in 2008 that she makes using regular soft 2B pencils which she keeps sharp. She begins in the top left, rubbing over an old art deco decorative glass panel, and works her way down to the bottom. The movements of her hand are regular, and evenly cover the whole surface, leaving no gaps. The result is the darkest grey, an almost black graphite surface, which has a definite sheen that is deep rather than bright like the highly reflective silver ones. In one example from the series (p.98) the smooth lead rays contrast with the densely-pitted pinhead pattern of frosted glass. In another, *Untitled (front door)* (2007, p.40), the larger lumpier texture of patterned glass is typical of the frosted inserts in 1970s' doors – in this case, a reconstruction of the front door of the artist's childhood home.

Her technique is reminiscent of the kind of rubbings children take of coins or wallpaper or tree barks, or of brass rubbing. Art historically, its precedent would seem to be the technique of making rubbings that the Surrealist artist Max Ernst called frottage. One of the things most often said about rubbing or frottage is that it is a direct transfer of one surface to another without the mediation of the conventions of representation. It is a way of imprinting the world without depicting it and so it is indexical – like a finger- or a footprint. And like a photograph too, or at least a pre-digital kind of photograph, where an image is imprinted on light-sensitive paper. It was the American philosopher Charles Sander Peirce who first put together this family set or category of images as a way of differentiating indexical from iconic, or conventionally depictive, images. But it has become part of our general understanding of how images work.

In some ways the indexical is a useful way of thinking about what holds Barriball's work together, although quite a lot of her work doesn't fit it – think of the buckets, or the plastic bag covered with red marker pen from 2000 (p.82). But, yes, there is a lot of 'resemblance by contact' – the transfer of surface to surface – of a kind that is thick with memory from 1930s' semis to 1970s' domestic interiors. But I suppose what becomes even more interesting in the work is what happens in the process – the radical dissimilarities that veer in all directions as a consequence of the techniques she likes using.

I wouldn't even call what Barriball does rubbing, let alone frottage. She doesn't leave any gaps. She entirely covers a sheet of paper and presses hard – hard enough that the sheet of paper moulds itself to the texture of whatever is beneath it – a bricked-up breeze block doorway (pp.44–45), say, or frosted glass (p.20). In a recent work, she took two arched shape shutters and pressed against their slats to make the paper itself undulate in waves and to bear the strain of that pressure (pp.22–24). The shutters had originally hung on a blank external wall on the back of a house to simulate (non-existent) windows. She has said that the two shutters attracted her partly because they reminded her of the blinking eyes of Betty Boop. The surface of them is no longer peeling paint but a black sheen, broken by innumerable little tears and pricks. And because the graphite is so dense and heavy, they have come to look darkly metallic, quite unlike their source. Just as inert breeze block comes to shine and refract the light, and frosted glass becomes heavy as lead.

Ernst wrote about his own discovery of frottage as an origin story for art: 'I made from the [floor]boards a series of drawings by placing on them, at random, sheets of paper which I undertook to rub with black lead. In gazing attentively at the drawings thus obtained … I was surprised by the sudden intensification of my visionary capacities'. It was as if vision became hallucinatory in the process allowing – inviting, demanding even – perceptual projections. So that when he made his frottages for the edition that he called *Natural History*, published as a set of photogravures in 1926, he juxtaposed lots of different impressions, from all sorts of different woods and patterned wallpapers, to make often fantastical images and imaginary landscapes.

I don't want to suggest that Barriball's drawings are literal by comparison – that a wall is simply a wall, a pane of frosted glass is a pane of frosted glass – because they are not. Mediated by the palpable layer of paper – wood, concrete, glass or brick all transform into materials that are not themselves but shiny, reflective and metallic. Maybe it is another kind of natural history of vision – one where that kind of projection is blocked in order to allow a more fully tactile and bodily type of looking.

The American poet Elizabeth Bishop once owned a set of Ernst's *Natural History*. She later said that the writing of her poem 'The Monument' had been influenced by it. She had wanted to write a poem that was a frottage of the sea. If Ernst's heightened vision isn't quite Barriball's, Bishop's reading of his frottages – for her own ends it has to be said – is perhaps more telling. The poem, included in her first volume of poems *North and South*, published in 1946, is full of wood. There is 'a sea of narrow, horizontal boards'. The sea 'looks made of wood, half-shining, like a driftwood sea'. The sky 'looks wooden, grained with cloud'. The poem itself is a kind of frottage, which picks up the movements and rhythms of the sea's agitated surface through the 'woodiness' of the words.

This is the point: the movement, the rhythm, the light. Not the tracing of the images so much as the sense of tracing a set of repetitive movements – like trying to mark the movement of something as structureless as the sea. After all, in addition to the rubbings over a given texture, the intricacy of Barriball's metallic surfaces comes about through the process of making

itself; the tiny tears in the paper, the crinkles, the rucks, the slight billows and bulges that come about. The final line of Bishop's poem asks us to 'Watch it closely'. Watch the surface of Barriball's drawings closely and these are the movements which she traces – the slightest movements or sudden shifts that she calibrates and makes material.

One of the largest works she has made to date is *Untitled* (2009, p.43), a dense black drawing that she traced over a bricked-up door that formed part of the wall of her studio at the time. The image is blocked off, like the door itself, but opens onto another terrain of more abstract textures – albeit ones that follow the intricate patterns as found. The transformation is fairly dramatic – with the graphite returning the wall to a purely mineral state – one with complex strata where the courses of mortar would have been. Great shanks of barely distinguishable pencil marks rain downwards, diagonally, towards the floor, as if the work has its own internal gravitational logic, quite at odds with the original surface.

And even more striking, the uneven folds and hollows and creases produced by the hand pushing the pencil across the sheet create yet another layer of texture – one that marks out the drift of the process of the work's making. These rough undulations and agitations incline like the ridges left by the tide on sand, but also hint at some secret movement underneath the surface. The work ends up being grainless and groundless, and it is unclear in the end whether the pressure is coming from above or beneath. And light, plus the glass over the drawings, reflects off the graphite or the silver to collect its own reflections – so that more fleeting effects catch on its surface. There is something unyielding about the metallic finish, and yet yielding in the light effects that it creates. These effects are strange and uncanny, especially the metallic gleam that is neither light nor dark. Dark light, perhaps, or better, Bishop's 'half-shine'.

I said at the start that Barriball's work is more resilient than it seems. There is nothing very fragile about it, even though it often has incredible delicacy. The reason for this is quite concrete. After all a lot of the work seems to be about resistance of one sort or another – or at least about this give and take between yielding to pressure and resisting it. The resistance of a sheet of paper to a hand that presses down on it. If currents of air had been one of the materials out of which *Draw (fireplace)* was made, then the large-scale work *Untitled* (2011, pp.6–11) is made out of the cheap woven screens designed to serve as an obstacle to the gusts of wind that beset any British beach. At first, it looks relatively heavy compared with the lightness of much of her other work. Drawn over in black marker pen to largely but not completely obliterate the bright colour, it stands slightly away from the wall, harbouring the reflected coloured light from the stripes behind it. Even though it might look bulky it is just as slight, and just as much a mould of nothing more substantial than the air that it encloses.

This is not so different, then, from the slender rolls of paper painted in copper acrylic paint that are displayed propped against the wall (p.14). If Eva Hesse – another artist, like Manzoni, that Barriball first discovered at art school – used fibreglass to make casts of cardboard tubes and made latex drapes to hang between tall fibreglass poles in the 1960s – then here some of those same casual sculptural shapes have been translated into even more provisional and incomplete states. In the same vein, but dramatically different in effect, a large roll of paper painted dense black with Chinese ink is shown propped up in a corner. Having 'cast' the shape by wrapping herself up in the paper, its massive presence – bearing the impressed dents and creases of an uncanny and ghostly body – belies its actual weightlessness. Yet despite its dark bulk – and there is no denying the massiveness of it – it still looks like a sculpture that has drawn breath and buckled (the echoes of *Draw (fireplace)* are hard to avoid).

These kinds of disparities are everywhere in the work. Things become what they are not. Walls look back at you. Floors fall away. Spareness can be a powerful tool for an agitator. Small points of friction open onto unexpected shifts in perception, just as something as slight as a metallic glimmer can make the darkest, most looming surface create the most unpredictable kind of light. This creates an uncanny effect not so much because of some property inherent to particular objects – the doors and windows of a house, for instance, or an old photograph – but because the uncanny is a condition of viewing highly susceptible to suggestion. The almost invisible, or the possibility of a movement beyond a surface as much as in front, is likely to trigger the greatest disturbance within the field of vision.

*Untitled I*, 2004, ink and bubble mixture on found photograph

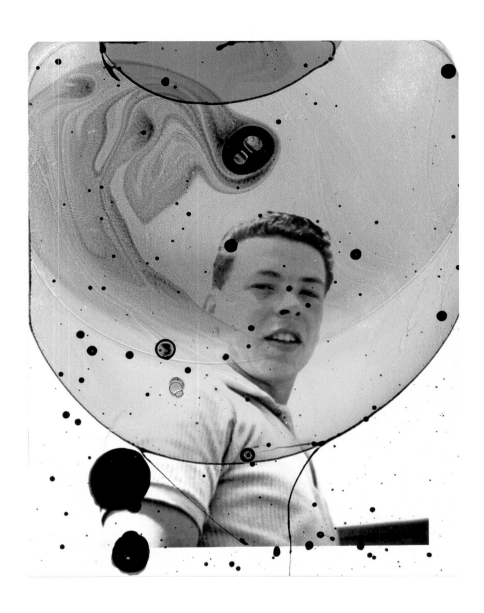

*Untitled VII*, 2004, ink and bubble mixture on found photograph

*Untitled I*, 2006, found slide, projector

Installation view, *Untitled II*, 2006, found slide, projector   67

68 *Untitled III*, 2006, found slide, projector

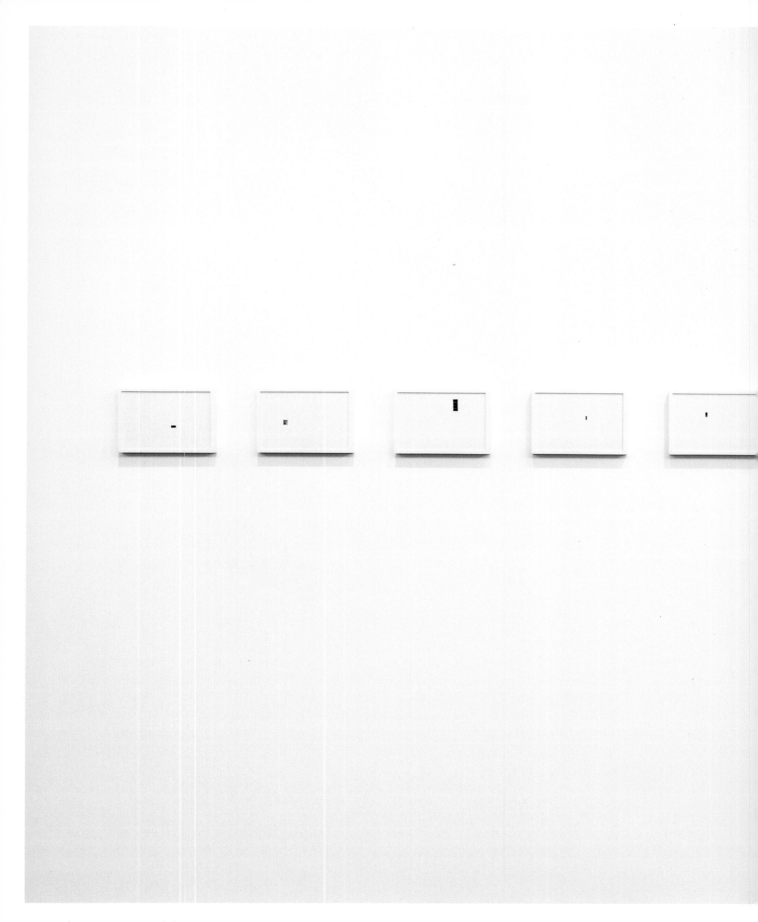

*Windows 1–10*, 2006, found photographs, paper

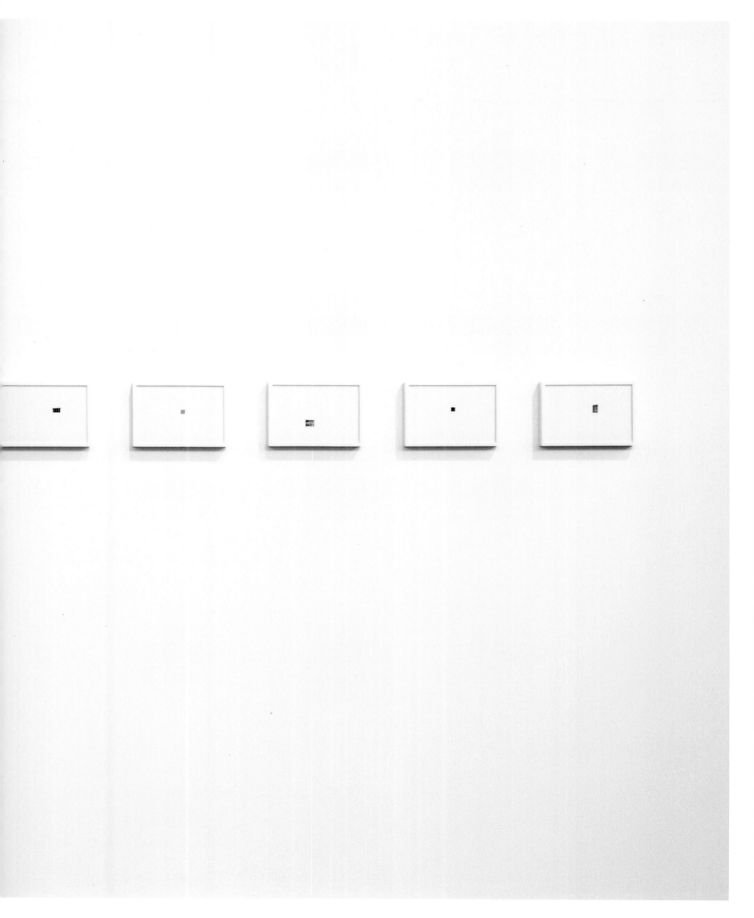

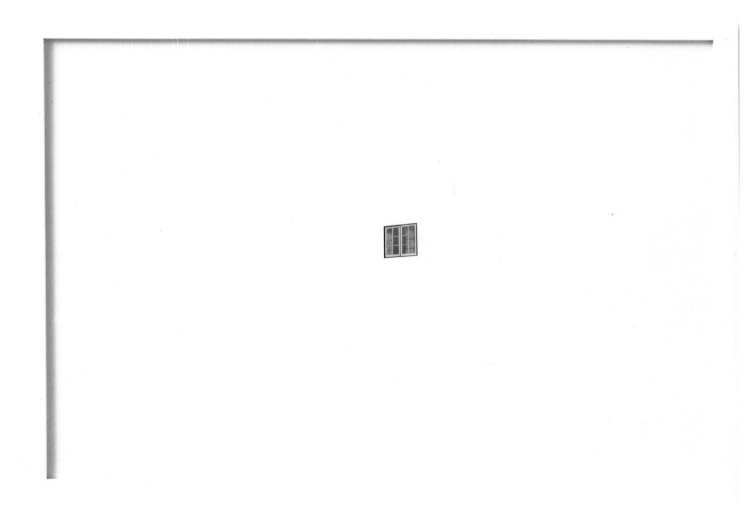

74 *Window 7*, 2006, found photograph, paper

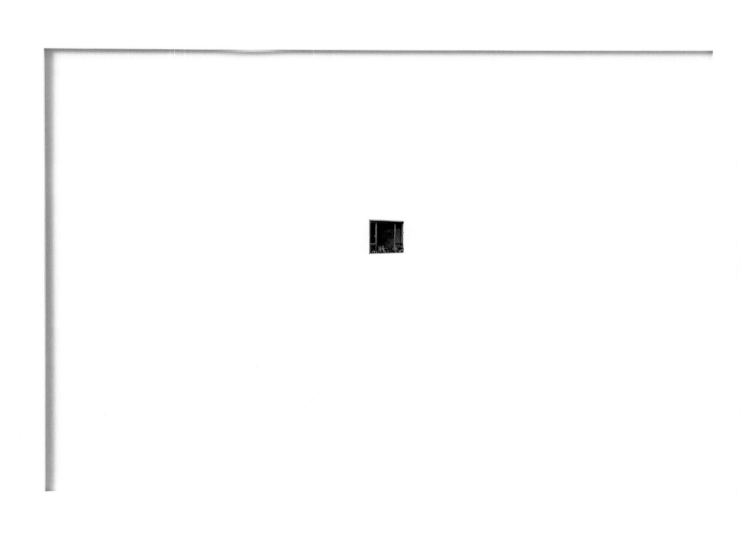

*Window 9*, 2006, found photograph, paper

*About 60 miles of beautiful views*, 2008, posters

# Oh, boy, what a wonderful city!

# About 60 miles of beautiful views.

MAYOR OF LONDON          Transport for London

# Off to work 8.15 AM. (Nylon uniform.)

MAYOR OF LONDON          Transport for London

MAYOR OF LONDON          Transport for London

# On way to birthday party.

# Looking back the way we had come.

MAYOR OF LONDON          Transport for London

# I THINK I'M BEING WATCHED.

MAYOR OF LONDON          Transport for London

MAYOR OF LONDON          Transport for London

The Way We Should Have Gone, 2010, inkjet print 81

82    *Bag drawing*, 2000, marker pen on carrier bag

84   *Light drawing*, 2000, marker pen on lamp and paper

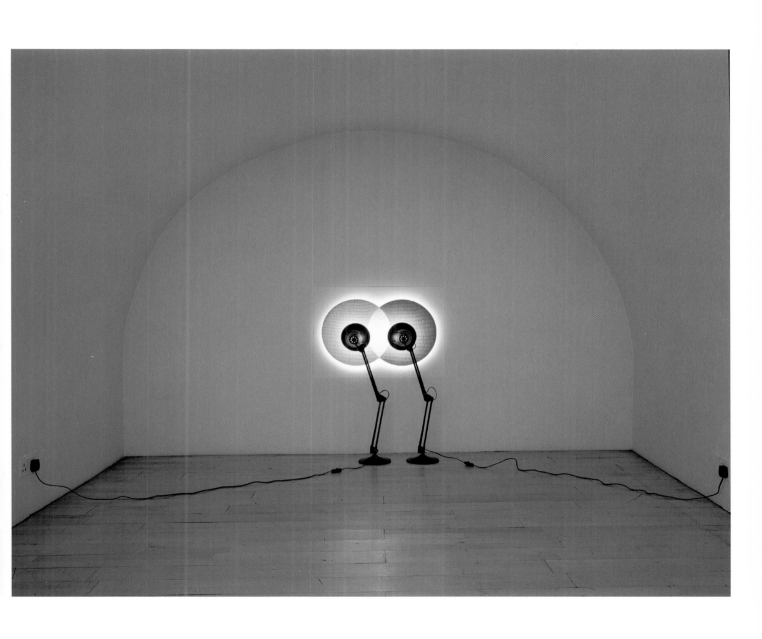

*Silver Map*, 2003, silver pen on world map   87

# IN CONVERSATION
## ANNA BARRIBALL / ANTHONY SPIRA

ANTHONY SPIRA (AS): *This book brings together a range of work made from 2000–2011, using drawing, sculpture, photography and video. There are consistent themes and interests throughout your practice, but could you describe your approach to different materials?*

ANNA BARRIBALL (AB): Initially at college, I was excited by materials like fabric, wax and paper. As well as drawings, I made works with paper dipped in sugar and wax or varnish which were very ephemeral. I was trying to make the materials behave in a way that they naturally wouldn't – a piece of fabric could stand up, but it didn't really want to.

AS: *Perhaps it was this interest in transformation that led to the process you often use of coating or covering an object in colour or with repetitive strokes.*

AB: *Bag drawing* (2000, p.82), was the last piece I made on my MA at Chelsea College of Art. It was a white carrier bag that I drew over inside and out with red marker pen. It's a very red, concentrated object. It describes its own form, while being both empty and full. Of course, there's the absurdity of spending so much time on a negligible, throwaway object but also an enjoyment in the contact, for example, between marker pen and polythene. Later in the same year

I made *Money drawing* (p.83), a five pound note that I drew over in gold pen. In some ways, my interest in changing values was more obvious in this piece. From a distance it looks like flat rolled gold, but close up you can see the embossed print, the creases where people have folded it or stuffed it into their pocket. The process of making it meant looking very closely and touching the whole surface.

AS: *What about* Silver Map *(2003, pp.86–87)?*

AB: This was a world map that I had on my wall for a few years that I decided to cover with silver pen. The process threw the printed map into relief under the surface – like oil on water. I was interested in the scale of the piece of paper in contrast to the scale of what it was describing, to create maybe a mirroring effect. And I was interested in the folds and incidental creases and marks pulling an image of the world back into the real world.

AS: *How did you shift from these everyday objects to making large-scale rubbings of architectural features including floorboards, walls with bricks of different kinds, windows, doors, etc.?*

AB: The first series of floorboards (*One Square Foot V*, 2001, pp.28–29) came about through moving to Berlin and feeling very dislocated in an exciting way. It was about being there at that time but also about trying to feel grounded. I was interested in the closeness of the drawing to the thing in the drawing. I wanted to avoid the space between looking and translation or representation so that it's as close as possible to the actual thing. There's a frustration about not being able to fully bridge that gap but if it moves any further apart then it doesn't ring true for me. The floorboards are more pictorial while later works became closer to, or more like, what they represent, like a door, section of wall or window. I was interested in moving from objects you look at to creating larger pieces that make you feel like you're in a space, and wanting the viewer to feel within the work, aware of their encounter with it.

AS: *The drawings lie somewhere between drawing, photography, facsimile or even a sculptural cast. But, primarily, they are related to capturing your experience of a particular place at a particular time in a very physical way.*

AB: My relationship to the work physically while making it has to be very close, involved and focused. There is a durational aspect to this work as well. The bricked-up door drawing (*Untitled*, 2009, p.43) was extreme to make, physically and mentally, because I was spending day after day inches away from a brick wall. It's unforgiving in lots of ways, but I do find it pleasurable. It also goes between being mindless and mindful, meditative and a form of endurance at the same time. With that drawing, I started up a ladder and worked my way down until I was lying flat on the floor. I liked that physical process even if it could feel quite claustrophobic.

AS: *What does this physical exertion, this performative, durational process bring to the work?*

AB: I hope it holds an energy, the intensity of its making. When you stand in front of it, the bricked-up doorway confronts you with its own making. But I also make work relatively quickly, for example, by using found objects – it might take a long period of thinking or searching, but the actual making can be very quick. Works such as *Untitled (80 slides)* (2005, p.71) bring a balance because I wouldn't want the idea of labour to override other aspects.

AS: *But you do specifically choose to work with quite fine pencils.*

AB: I use normal pencils and it's the point of the pencil that pushes the paper almost like a carving process. If I changed the scale of the point of the end of the pencil, then it would have a completely different feeling with much less detail. There is something about getting down to that very fine point that is important to the way the drawing feels in the end. I like the fact that it is a piece of paper and a pencil point, that it's the most basic drawing material.

AS: *There's also something quite obsessive, or at least totally absorbing about this process.*

AB: It's about engaging with something on a forensic level and using a process of heightened looking. I think it's an intuitive thing that relates to making a whole surface, so that no part the paper is left untouched. When the very last bit of the paper is covered, the drawing suddenly does something very different, it becomes its own thing. It becomes autonomous, yet it's a double. It becomes a sort of whole, something you can look at instantaneously, but that also breaks down the more you look at it because you see all the individual marks. It takes on a new character.

AS: *So, when looked at very closely, the specific time and place recorded in your drawings become destabilised by millions of tiny details. It seems that your work is concerned with a physical experience and emotional response to the world even though it is generally focused on the constructed environment.*

AB: The work often starts with finding something that triggers a memory and a personal experience. I am very aware of myself physically when I make these pieces, and you see a reflection of yourself in the surface or in the glass of the frame when you stand in front of them. So for me they are very much about the body and a physical, emotional experience.

AS: *Reflection has definitely played an understated role in your work. Can you describe the new piece using flash photography that has been produced for this show* Untitled *(2011, pp.93–95) ?*

AB: I took a series of flash photographs at night in different interiors looking through windows. I used the autofocus so that I didn't know what the camera would focus on – it might be a mark on the surface of the glass, or perhaps my hand in reflection, or the light of the flash reflected back and recorded. I liked the surprise of it. Sometimes the sudden harsh illumination flooded the image and produced quite spectral effects. I decided to have the images intermittently flashing on a monitor in intervals like blinking. Inverting the images means that the dark becomes light and vice versa. The images flash very quickly and you aren't sure what you are looking at or what you've seen. There is a ghosting and an afterimage. It also feels like you have something in your eye. I wanted to create an awareness of looking, a moment of recognition that goes beyond the literal. I was amazed how this piece seems to contain a lot of other works: the windows of the found photograph series (*Windows 1–10*, 2006, pp.72–77), and the marks of the ink and bubble mixture blown onto photographs from 2004 (*Untitled I–XII*, pp.13, 62–65) are echoed in it. Video, photography and drawing cross over and blur which I feel very excited about. It was the last piece that came together for the exhibition at MK Gallery; a fusing of things to take forward.

AS: *You have made other video works, which also draw attention to our physicality, bringing what you call an awareness of looking or moment of recognition. How did they come about?*

AB: They have both come about as a result of happenstance. For *Draw (fireplace)* (2005, pp.53, 54, 57), I was moving out of a flat and had always liked the tiles on the fireplace and the floor. I was intending to make tracings of them as a personal record and placed the tracing paper up over the fireplace. It was a windy day and the fireplace started breathing, sucking in and blowing the paper out. I was mesmerised and sat there watching this scene for quite some time. For *Projection* (2003, pp.50–51), I was looking out of the window in my sister's flat and sunlight was bouncing off a sequinned t-shirt I was wearing and onto the wall. You could see my heartbeat and my breathing in the movement of the reflected light – a picture of what was happening inside was projected externally. We caught it on my sister's video camera.

AS: *In some ways, your drawings have a similar effect by tracing the natural and often overlooked 'life' of objects, highlighting the wear and tear of the everyday, but could you talk about your work with photography in relation to physicality, and more specifically, breathing?*

AB: *36 Breaths* (2002, pp.60–61), is a work made with photographs I found in a market, of a family on holiday. I had them in my studio for a long time and I would look at them without really knowing what I wanted to do with them, if anything. In the end I let fall a single drop of ink as near to the centre of each individual photograph as possible and then blew each drop. I was thinking at that time, in contrast to the pencil drawings, of making 'hands-off' works where I had no physical contact. There was also an odd contrast of re-animating the images whilst also obliterating them slightly, and I feed off contrast and opposites. I went on from that to make the bubble pieces, mixing ink with bubble mixture and blowing this onto photographs, so that again there was no direct touch involved . But there was a layer of my time and a layer of my presence on top of these found images. I was aware that the bursting of the bubble mirrored the click of the camera shutter. Within this there is a desire to hold something still and look hard, a kind of preservation. I was also interested in the layering of time – the ink marks draw attention to the pictures' surface bringing these images from the past back as real objects in the present. I was also looking for an element of surprise or accident to see how something turns out within a process that isn't definitive.

AS: *It seems that the action you describe as a bursting bubble or clicking shutter also replicates the blinking action you mentioned in the new flash photography piece. They seem to be different mechanisms for freezing an image or capturing a moment. This impulse to give a fixed, tangible quality to fleeting and elusive memories and moments stands in stark contrast with the more spontaneous discoveries that you have described which channel natural forces with little or no physical contact.*

AB: There are moments in the studio when you think you are doing one thing and then something happens to lead you in another direction. Things often come together through accident or on the periphery of making, as for example with the standing or leaning pieces from 2008 made with ink on paper (*Untitled II*, *Untitled III*, pp.12, 15). When I was making a large drawing on the wall of my studio, I covered the sheet of paper in ink and went over the surface with a rubber to pick up the texture of the wall. I wanted the drawing not to lie flat but to start peeling away from the wall, to lift into the space of the viewer. I covered the back of the drawing in ink so you could no longer see any exposed paper, transforming it materially. Then I moved the drawing to work on something else, intending to return to it another time. Unselfconsciously I rolled it and stood it in the corner of the studio to free up wall space. In taking it off the wall and standing it in the corner the drawing had taken on an unpredictable, very different and strange presence. It had weight although it was a thin sheet of paper covered in ink. It was hard to describe exactly what it was. It's exciting when you stop and notice things on the way and allow the work to change direction.

AS: *To some extent, the appearance of your large-scale new work,* Untitled *(2011, pp.6–11) is also open to chance as the level of saturation of black ink on the shop-bought windbreaks is determined as the pens run dry and are replaced by new ones. The effect of light, and how it moves and changes, is also crucial as in so much of your work.*

AB: The drawing moves across the surface like a weather front, from left to right. The colours fade in and out so that the pen seems to add more colour, while also obscuring the work in an odd way. This piece stands a little away from the wall and the space behind creates a rainbow of sorts, produced by light travelling through the coloured plastic onto the wall. Where the windbreak material doesn't quite meet, slatted light comes through.

AS: *Aside from light, though, you also use air, wind, breath and the elements in general in a lot of your work.*

AB: I am drawn to the unfixed quality, the destabilising feeling that things can shift or even disappear; the sense of movement. The rhythm of breathing is echoed in the rhythm of the drawings. Time, air and light become materials in the work, animating either the space or the thing itself.

AS: *You have also recently been using photography to similar effect, such as in* Detail *(2011, pp.5, 19), where you blow up details from small, found photographs so that all the dirt and blemishes on the surface are amplified in a way that appears to dissolve the original image. It sometimes seems that the photographs you use become increasingly like drawings, while the drawings become more like photographs.*

AB: I'm surprised by how much the language I use when talking about my work relates to photography – apertures, exposure, shutters, for example – and I'm interested in the relationship between photography, drawing and memory. The process of recording, remembering and revisiting; creating documents that provide evidence for something more elusive.

AS: *Could you talk more about the new large photograph* Detail?

AB: *Detail* is from a found photograph of a formal group portrait. On the left edge of the original image is a window with a mysterious, obscured presence behind. I isolated the window and enlarged it to life-size to see what you could see within the given information. What is incidental and on the periphery is brought into focus. The glass and picture frame mimic the window frame in the image. I wanted all the visual noise accumulated on the original photograph, and also generated by the process of scanning and enlarging the image. This interference or disturbance within the image also illustrates the lifespan of the photograph.

AS: *The doubling of the mirror and window frames in* Detail *(like the playful 'window mounts' in the earlier* Windows *series also serves to close that gap you described earlier between the subject and how it is represented. Also, like the drawing* Window *(2002, p.20), in which the viewer's face is inevitably reflected, these pieces call into question the viewer's position. Likewise, the placement of* Detail, *high up on a wall, creates an unnerving sense that you are being watched from a first floor window.*

AB: I am interested in the presence that a piece of work can have. In this case there is an implied presence behind the surface of the glass. Installed at first floor height its placement is plausible. You might not notice the window immediately, a bit like when you sense someone is looking at you, which makes you turn to look at them. I am interested in the confusion of being inside or outside, in a liminal space. Thresholds that are no longer ways in or ways out – drawings that hold you in the space while hinting at what might be behind the surface.

AS: *And also in the confusion between making familiar objects or surfaces unfamiliar – is this part of what gives the work a sense of the Freudian uncanny? Perhaps the literal translation of Freud's term 'unheimlich', 'unhomely', is appropriate, particularly with works that play with domestic themes.*

AB: I am interested in how the domestic can heighten the familiar and the strange. I grew up in a 1970s' semi-detached house, next door to my best friend whose house was a mirror image of mine. While I was thinking about making a show at Frith Street Gallery in London, I came across a pair of curtains in a market that were the same as the curtains in the house where I grew up. I had been thinking about the floor of the gallery which is concrete, the kind of floor you would find in an outside space. I wanted to cut the leaves free from the pattern, liberate them from the fabric. Once they were cut out, the shapes behaved like leaves. I collected a lot of second-hand curtains, which all carried memories of a life in someone's house to make the floor piece which plays on ideas of interior and exterior space. With *Yellow Leaves* (2011, pp.16–17) I have only used the cartoon-like leaves from the original found curtains that sparked the memory.

AS: *It seems appropriate to consider memory as another form of doubling, like photography or tracing, and it's interesting that childhood memories play a role in your work, as the process you use has certain child-like associations of 'colouring- in', for example. But at the same time, the schematised, cartoon-like quality of the leaves couldn't be further from the detail and intensity of the drawings. Maybe the new* Shutters *(2011, pp.22–24) piece where the paper has been chiselled, torn and pushed to its limits, while looking like a blank pair of cartoon eyes from a distance, is another example of these contrasts that, as you say, you continuously feed off throughout your work.*

AB: I like using processes that are low-fi and accessible, that we can all do and remember engaging with and enjoying – colouring-in, blowing bubbles, taking rubbings from coins, processes that take the pressure off making things, making 'art'. The contrasts provide a precarious balance of opposites which, going back to your earlier question about the Freudian uncanny, is also found in the term 'unheimlich', the unhomely, which relies on the coexistence of the homely.

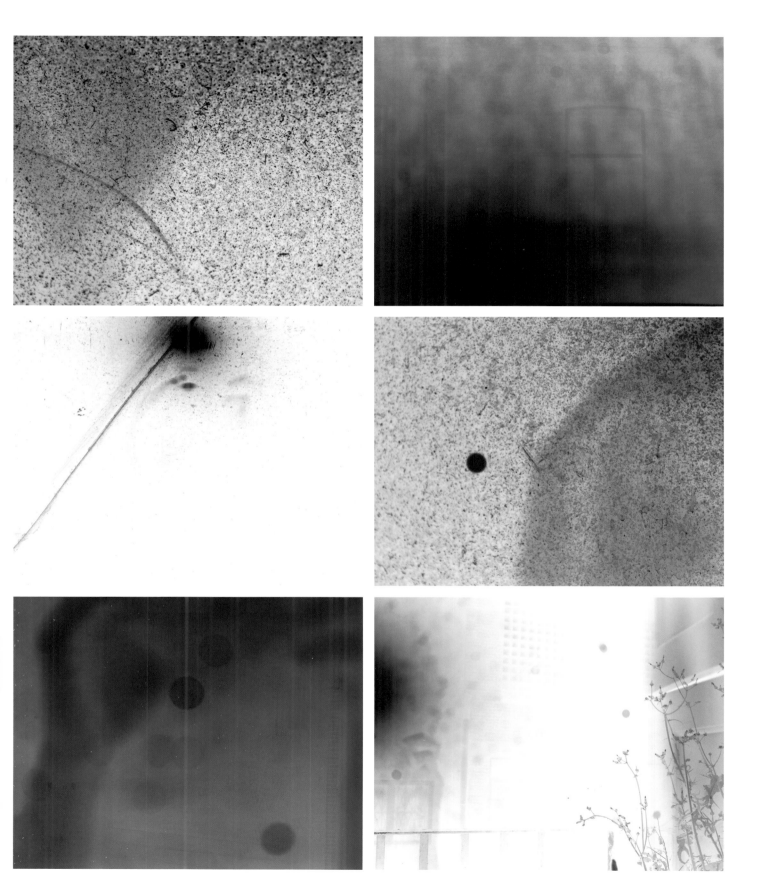

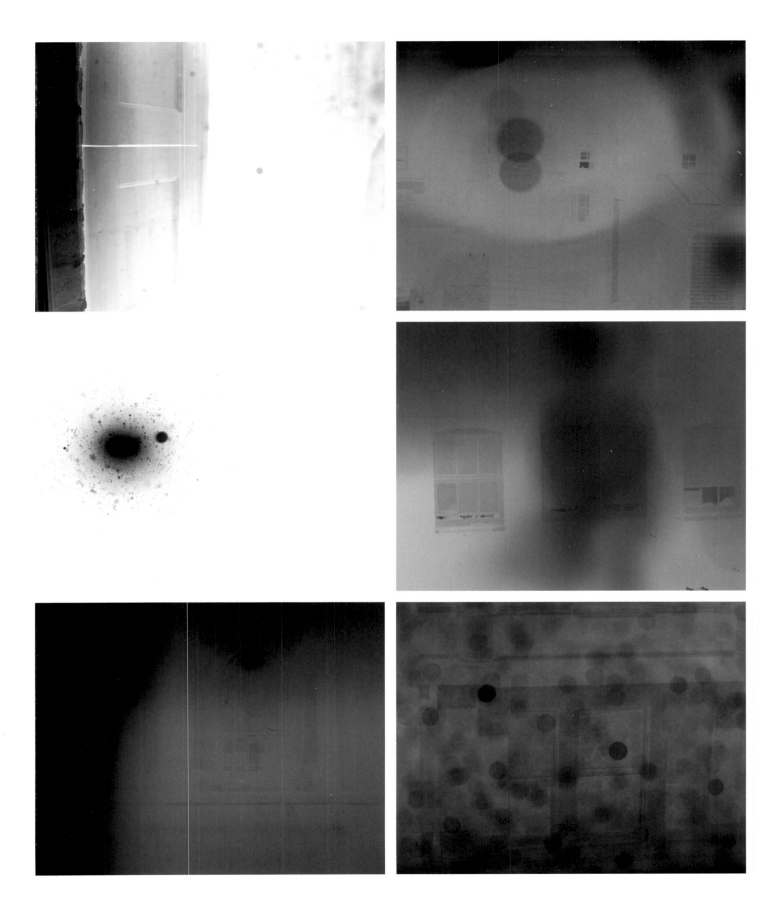

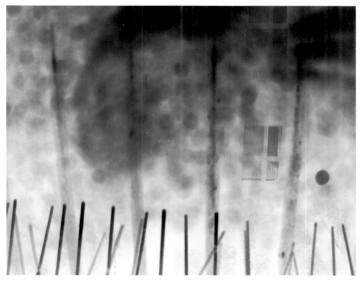

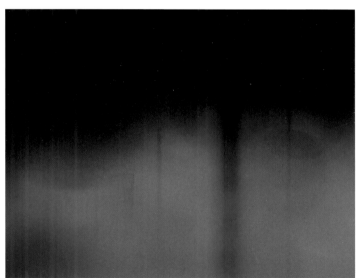

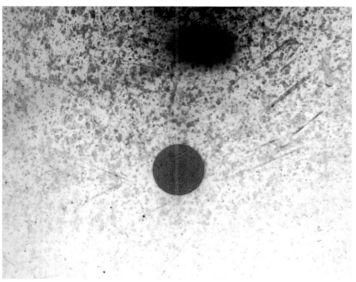

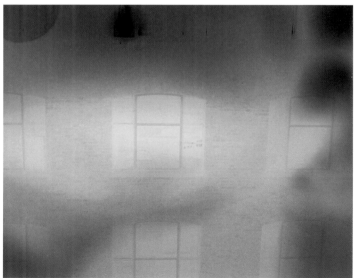

*Sunrise/Sunset VIII*, 2010, pencil on paper

# PLATE LIST

All sizes given framed, h x w x d

pages 5, 19
*Detail*, 2011
Silver gelatin print
135 x 91 cm
Courtesy the artist and
Frith Street Gallery, London

pages 6–11
*Untitled*, 2011
Marker pen on windbreaks,
metal poles
Dimensions variable
Courtesy the artist and
Frith Street Gallery, London

page 12
*Untitled III*, 2008
Ink on paper
239 x 36 x 29 cm
Courtesy the artist and
Frith Street Gallery, London

page 13, 64
*Untitled VII*, 2004
Ink and bubble mixture
on found photograph
34 x 25 cm
Collection of Sandra
and Giancarlo Bonollo

pages 13, 63
*Untitled V*, 2004
Ink and bubble mixture
on found photograph
34 x 25 cm
Collection of Sandra
and Giancarlo Bonollo

pages 13, 65
*Untitled XII*, 2004
Ink and bubble mixture
on found photograph
34 x 25 cm

Collection of Karon Hepburn
and Freddie Baveystock

page 14
*Copper Pipes*, 2011
Acrylic paint on paper
122 x 4 x 4 cm; 122 x 3 x 3 cm
Courtesy the artist and
Frith Street Gallery, London

page 15
*Untitled II*, 2008
Ink on paper
239 x 66 x 22 cm
Courtesy the artist and
Frith Street Gallery, London

pages 15, 16–17, 19
*Yellow Leaves*, 2011
Curtain fabric
Dimensions variable
Courtesy the artist and
Frith Street Gallery, London

pages 19, 38
*Door*, 2004
Pencil on paper
209 x 88 x 6 cm
The Saatchi Gallery, London

page 20
*Window*, 2002
Pencil on paper
56 x 51 cm
Arts Council Collection,
Southbank Centre, London

page 21
*Silver Curtain*, 2011
Slash curtain
250 x 91 cm
Courtesy the artist and
Frith Street Gallery, London

pages 22–24
*Shutters*, 2011
Diptych, pencil on paper
182 x 131 cm each
Private collection, New York

pages 28–29
*One Square Foot V*, 2001
Pencil on paper
31 x 31 cm
Collection of Mr & Mrs Stefano
Pansera

page 30
*Knife II*, 2004
Cotton and paper
46 x 36 cm
Private collection

page 31
*Black Wardrobe*, 2003
Tape on wardrobe
178 x 70 x 40 cm
The Saatchi Gallery, London

pages 32–33
*Mirror Window Wall I*, 2008
Ink on paper
261 x 201 cm
Courtesy the artist and
Frith Street Gallery, London

page 35
*Brick Wall*, 2005
Pencil on paper
76 x 106 x 4 cm
Tate: Purchased using
funds provided by the 2006
Outset / Frieze Art Fair
Fund to benefit the
Tate Collection 2007

pages 36–37
*Wall Mirrors*, 2007
Diptych, silver pencil on paper
113 x 83 cm each
Lodeveans Collection

page 39
*Untitled*, 2007
Pencil on paper
209 x 95 cm
Private collection

page 40
*Untitled (front door)*, 2007
Pencil on paper
127 x 92 cm; 66 x 92 cm
Courtesy Galleri Bo Bjerggaard,
Copenhagen

page 41
*Untitled (back door)*, 2006
Pencil on paper
113 x 71 cm
Collection of Charles Asprey

page 43
*Untitled*, 2009
Pencil on paper
218 x 134 cm
Private collection

pages 44–45
*Untitled*, 2010
Silver pencil on black paper
200 x 123 cm
Private collection

page 46
*Green Glass*, 2008
Ink on paper
58 x 49 cm
Courtesy the artist and
Frith Street Gallery, London

page 47
*Textured Glass*, 2010
Ink on paper
58 x 49 cm
Courtesy the artist and
Frith Street Gallery, London

page 48
*Shutters with Fire Red*, 2011
Pencil, paper, acrylic spray
paint on board
82 x 97 cm
Alex Dellal Collection

page 49
*Silver Door with Fire Red*, 2011
Ink, paper, acrylic spray
paint on board
213 x 95 cm
Private collection

pages 50–51
*Projection*, 2003
Video projection
5 mins 54 secs
Courtesy the artist and
Frith Street Gallery, London

pages 53, 54, 57
*Draw (fireplace)*, 2005
Video projection
10 mins 30 secs
Courtesy the artist and
Frith Street Gallery, London;
Collection of HEART
– Herning Museum of
Contemporary Art, Herning

pages 60–61
*36 Breaths*, 2002
Ink on found photographs
46 x 46 cm
Collection of Octavius
and Joanne Black

page 62
*Untitled I*, 2004
Ink and bubble mixture
on found photograph
34 x 25 cm
Courtesy the artist and
Frith Street Gallery, London

page 66
*Untitled I*, 2006
Found slide, projector
Dimensions variable
Courtesy the artist and
Frith Street Gallery, London

page 67
*Untitled II*, 2006
Found slide, projector
Dimensions variable
Courtesy the artist and
Frith Street Gallery, London

page 68
*Untitled III*, 2006
Found slide, projector
Dimensions variable
Tate: Purchased using funds
provided by the 2006 Outset /
Frieze Art Fair Fund to benefit
the Tate Collection 2007

page 69
*Untitled IV*, 2006
Found slide, projector
Dimensions variable
Courtesy the artist and
Frith Street Gallery, London

*Untitled V*, 2006
Found slide, projector
Dimensions variable
Tate: Purchased using funds
provided by the 2006 Outset /
Frieze Art Fair Fund to benefit
the Tate Collection 2007

page 71
*Untitled (80 slides)*, 2005
Found slides, tape
5 x 5 x 23 cm
Courtesy the artist and
Frith Street Gallery, London

pages 72–77
*Windows 1–10*, 2006
Found photographs, paper
19 x 27 cm each
Private collection, courtesy
Galleri Bo Bjerggaard,
Copenhagen

pages 78–79
From the series
*About 60 miles of beautiful
views*, commissioned by
Art on the Underground, 2008
DR poster, 102 x 64 cm
Escalator poster, 57 x 42 cm
Foursheet poster, 152 x 102 cm

page 81
*The Way We Should Have
Gone*, 2010
Inkjet print
238 x 168 cm
Part of *Hey We're Closed!*
Hayward Gallery
Closure Programme
Courtesy Hayward Gallery,
Southbank Centre, London

page 82
*Bag drawing*, 2000
Marker pen on carrier bag
45 x 38 x 21 cm
Colección Bergé, Spain

page 83
*Money drawing*, 2000
Gold pen on five pound note
26 x 34 cm
Private collection

page 84
*Light drawing*, 2000
Marker pen on lamp and paper
Dimensions variable
Courtesy the artist and
Frith Street Gallery, London

page 85
*green + blue = cyan*, 2001
Marker pen on lamps and paper
Dimensions variable
British Council Collection

pages 86–87
*Silver Map*, 2003
Silver pen on world map
83 x 132 cm
Leeds Museums and Galleries
(purchased through the
Contemporary Art Society's

Special Collection Scheme on
behalf of Leeds Art Gallery
with Lottery funding from
Arts Council England, 2005)

pages 93–95
*Untitled*, 2011
Video loop, monitor
Courtesy the artist and
Frith Street Gallery, London

page 97
*The Night*, 2000
Digital pigment print on paper
172 x 270 cm
Courtesy the artist and
Frith Street Gallery, London

page 98
*Sunrise/Sunset VIII*, 2010
Pencil on paper
56 x 40 cm
Private collection

page 99
*Sunrise/Sunset V*, 2008
Pencil on paper
85 x 55 cm each
Arts Council Collection
Southbank Centre, London

pages 100–103
Installation views
Frith Street Gallery, London

# ANNA BARRIBALL

Born in Plymouth, 1972. Lives and works in London

## EDUCATION

1999–2000 Chelsea College of Art, MA Fine Art, London
1992–1995 Winchester School of Art, BA (Hons), Fine Art
1991–1992 Falmouth School of Art, Foundation Studies

## SOLO EXHIBITIONS

2011 MK Gallery, Milton Keynes; The Fruitmarket Gallery, Edinburgh*
2009 Frith Street Gallery, London
2008 *Projection*, Institut im Glaspavillon, Berlin
2007 *Live Art Performance: More and More – Performance of Reduction*, Artist Studio Residency, Camden Arts Centre, London
Galleri Bo Bjerggaard, Copenhagen*
2006 Ingleby Gallery, Edinburgh
The New Art Gallery, Walsall
2005 Gasworks, London; Newlyn Art Gallery, Cornwall*
2004 Frith Street Gallery, London
2003 *Recognition: Anna Barriball and David Musgrave*, Arnolfini, Bristol*

## SELECTED GROUP EXHIBITIONS

2011 *Outrageous Fortune: Artists Remake the Tarot*, Hayward Touring Exhibition: Focal Point Gallery, Southend-on-Sea; Queens Hall Arts Centre, Hexham; Jersey Arts Centre, St. Helier; mac, Birmingham; Holden Gallery, Manchester; University of Hertfordshire Galleries; Bedales Gallery, Petersfield; Arts Centre East Kilbride; Rhyl Library*
2010 *GOTTA GETTAWAY*, Quare, London
*Hey We're Closed!*, Hayward Gallery, London
*Newspeak: British Art Now: Part Two*, The Saatchi Gallery, London*

*Permanent Mimesis: An Exhibition on Realism and Simulation*, GAM Torino, Turin*
*Acute Melancholia*, Studio 44, Stockholm
2009 *Lunar Distance*, De Hallen Haarlem*
*Timewarp*, CRAC Alsace, Altkirch
*Second Hand*, Engholm Engelhorn Gallery, Vienna
2008 *About 60 miles of beautiful views*, commissioned by Art on the Underground, London
*Park Avenue*, Southampton City Art Gallery
*Prospects and Interiors: Sculptors' drawings*, Henry Moore Institute/Leeds City Art Gallery
*Out Riding Feet*, Harris Liebermann, New York
2007 *Echo Room: Art From Britain*, Alcalá 31, Madrid*
*SCARY MOVIE*, Contemporary Art Centre of South Australia, Adelaide*
2006 *Resonance: The Final Exhibition at 59–60 Frith Street*, Frith Street Gallery, London
*How to Improve the World: 60 Years of British Art*, Hayward Gallery, London*
*I Walk the Lines*, Galerie Barbara Thumm, Berlin
*Until It Makes Sense: Drawing As A Time Based Medium*, Seventeen Gallery, London; Galerie Thaddaeus Ropac, Paris*
*You'll Never Know: Drawing and Random Interference*, Hayward Touring Exhibition: Harris Museum and Art Gallery, Preston; Glynn Vivian Gallery, Swansea; The Lowry, Salford; The New Art Gallery, Walsall; Tullie House Museum and Art Gallery, Carlisle*
2005 *British Art Show 6*, BALTIC Centre for Contemporary Art, Gateshead; Manchester; Nottingham; Bristol*
*The Hardest Thing to Draw is a Kiss*, Wimbledon College of Art, London
2003 *Frequencies*, Frith Street Gallery, London
*Turpentine*, Studio Voltaire, London
*Bonobos*, Niels Borch Jensen Galerie, Berlin
*Not Always The Same*, Hammer Sidi, London; Mjellby Art Centre, Halmstad
2002 *STILL LIFE in contemporary British art*, Museo Nacional de Bellas Artes, Santiago; Caracas; Buenos Aires; Rosario;

Mexico City; Bogotá; Panama City; Guatemala City; São Paulo; Rio de Janeiro*

*Superfluity: British Artists at Latvijas Makslas Akadēmija*, Riga

*Pizza Express Prospects Drawing Prize*, Essor Gallery Project Space, London

2001 *Giardino*, Centro Culturale Paggeria del Comune di Sassuolo, Modena; Studio d'arte Raffaelli, Trento; Galleria del Tasso arte contemporanea, Bergamo

*The (Ideal)*, *Home Show*, Gimpel Fils, London

*Drawings*, Frith Street Gallery, London

*Rewind*, Glassbox, Paris

2000 *Felt-tip*, Zwemmer Gallery, London

*Oeuvre d'etre/Works of Being*, Temple Gallery, Rome

*Bloomberg New Contemporaries 2000*, MK Gallery, Milton Keynes; Cornerhouse, Manchester; Inverleith House, Edinburgh*

*The Armchair Project*, Cinch, London

*Here Comes the Night*, 15c St Charles Square, London

*Living With the Dutch*, 89a Erlanger Road, London

1999 *The Office of Misplaced Events*, Lotta Hammer Gallery, London

*Brainstorm*, Goldsmiths College, London

*Equinox*, Cairn Gallery, Nailsworth

1997 *ne me quitte pas*, Glassbox, Paris

1995 *Works on Paper*, The Brooks Centre, Winchester

* denotes catalogue

# BIBLIOGRAPHY

PUBLICATIONS

2011   *Anna Barriball* (texts: Fiona Bradley, Briony Fer,
       In Conversation Anna Barriball, Anthony Spira),
       MK Gallery, Milton Keynes and The Fruitmarket Gallery,
       Edinburgh
       *Outrageous Fortune Tarot Deck*, Slimvolume Poster
       Publication, London

2010   *Permanent Mimesis: An Exhibition about Simulation and
       Realism* (texts: Alessandro Rabottini, Seth Price, Sterling
       Ruby), Electa Mondadori, Milan
       *Newspeak: British Art Now: From The Saatchi Gallery,
       London* (foreword: Patricia Ellis), Booth-Clibborn Editions,
       London

2009   *Lunar Distance/The Knight's Tour* (texts: Arie Altena, Nickel
       van Duijvenboden, Xander Karskens, Mariska Kriek, Suzanne
       Wallinga), De Hallen Haarlem
       *Timewarp* (text: Felicity Lunn), CRAC Alsace, Altkirch
       *Obsession: Contemporary Art from the Lodeveans Collection*,
       (texts: John and Stuart Evans, Layla Bloom), The Stanley &
       Audrey Burton Gallery, University of Leeds

2008   *Order. Desire. Light.* (texts: Enrique Juncosa, Paolo Colombo,
       Catherine Lampert), Irish Museum of Modern Art, Dublin

2007   *Echo Room: Art from Britain* (texts: JJ Charlesworth,
       Victoria Combalía), British Council, London
       *Anna Barriball* (text: Richard Grayson), Galleri Bo Bjerggaard,
       Copenhagen
       *Bergé Collection* (text: Javier García Montes), Bergé
       *SCARY MOVIE* (text: Richard Grayson), Contemporary Art
       Centre of South Australia, Adelaide

2006   *How To Improve The World: 60 Years of British Art*,
       (texts: Michael Archer, Marjorie Allthorpe-Guyton,
       Roger Malbert), Hayward Publishing, London
       *Until It Makes Sense: Drawing As A Time Based Medium*,
       (text: James Brooks), Seventeen Gallery, London and
       Galerie Thaddaeus Ropac, Paris
       *You'll Never Know: Drawing and Random Interference*,
       (texts: Henry Krokatsis, Jeni Walwin, James Flint,
       Janna Levin, Sally O'Reilly), Hayward Publishing, London

2005   *Vitamin D: New Perspectives in Drawing*, Phaidon Press,
       London
       *British Art Show 6* (texts: Alex Farquharson, Andrea Schlieker),
       Hayward Publishing, London
       *Anna Barriball* (text: Ian Hunt), Gasworks Gallery, London
       and Newlyn Art Gallery, Cornwall

2003   *Recognition: Anna Barriball, David Musgrave, Edwina Ashton,
       David Mackintosh* (text: Sacha Craddock), Arnolfini, Bristol

2002   *STILL LIFE* (text: Ann Gallagher), British Council, London

2000   *Bloomberg New Contemporaries 2000* (texts: discussion
       between Sarah Kent, Jeremy Millar, Sacha Craddock,
       Des Lawrence), New Contemporaries Ltd., London


SELECTED ARTICLES

2011   Amy Pettifer, 'Let me in', *goodgreyday.blogspot.com*,
       October

2010   Sara d' Alessandro, 'Paradoxical Skin', *MAG*, Magazine d'Arte
       Della GAM, September
       Helen Sumpter, 'Charles Saatchi unveils a new Britart
       generation', *Time Out*, 11–17 November
       Laura McLean-Ferris, 'Newspeak: British Art Now, Part 2,
       Saatchi Gallery London', *Independent*, 12 November

2009   Laura McLean-Ferris, 'Review', *Art Monthly*, March
       Eliza Williams, 'Review', *Flash Art*, March
       Chris Fite-Wassilak, 'Focus – Anna Barriball', *Frieze*, April
       Rebecca Geldard, 'Review', *Modern Painters*, April
       Vivian Millet, 'CRAC Alsace: Les artistes explorent le temps',
       June
       Helen Sumpter, 'New Work', *Art World*, June/July
       Nicolas Lehr, 'L'espace du temps', *DNA Reflets*, July
       'The Artist: Anna Barriball', *Maybourne*, Autumn/Winter

2008   Tim Stott, 'Reviews', *Art Review*, January
       Kira Hesser, 'Oh Boy! New Art on the Underground',
       *Londonist*, June
       Ken Russell, 'More art on the Underground', *Times 2*, July
       Christy Lange, 'Events', *Frieze*, November–December

2007 Eliza Williams, 'You'll Never Know: Drawing and Random
Interference', Review, *Art Monthly*, February
Tim Stott, Clarke & McDevitt, *Art Review*, March
Almudena Baeza, 'New British Art', *El Mundo*, April
Nacho Santos, 'La ca mara de eco', April
Carlos Jiménez, 'La razón desvaída', *El Pais (Babelia)*, April
Marianne Novarro, Ecos de la Moderndad, *El Cultural*, June
Lisbeth Bonde, *Kunst Og Kød*, September
2006 Neil Mulholland and Andrew Hunt, 'British Art (does It),
Show?' *Frieze*, January/February
Martin Coomer, 'Vitamin D', *Time Out*, February
David Barrett, 'Until it makes sense', *Art Monthly*, June
WB, 'Anna Barriball', *Metro*, July
2005 Craig Burnett, 'Anna Barriball', *Time Out*, 1–8 June
Martin Holman, 'Anna Barriball', Newlyn Art Gallery,
*Galleries*, September
Adrian Searle, 'State of the art', *Guardian*, 27 September
2004 Martin Herbert, 'Anna Barriball', *Time Out*, April
Peter Chapman, 'Anna Barriball', *Independent*, April
Jessica Lack, 'Picks of the Week: Anna Barriball', *Guardian*,
3 May
Mark Godfrey, 'Anna Barriball', *Frieze*, June/July/August
2003 Yasmin Monsalve, 'Naturaleza muerta recreada', *Temp Libre*,
April
Simon Villamizar, 'Naturaleza muerta contemporanea en el
MBA', *El Mundo*, May
Melissa Oberto Limongi, 'Reino Unido y Venezuela dialogan
sobre Naturaleza muerta', *El Sacional*, May
Tom Phillips, 'Gang of four', *Venue*, 16–22 May
Jessica Lack, 'Anna Barriball & David Musgrave, Arnolfini,
Preview', *The Guardian*, The Guide, 17–23 May
Jessica Lack, 'Frequencies, Preview', *The Guardian*, The Guide,
24–30 May
'As seen by...', *Time Out*, 4–11 June
Martin Coomer, 'Frequencies', *Time Out*, 11–18 June
'Anna Barriball & David Musgrave, Arnolfini', *Art Review*,
June
Sally O'Reilly, 'Profile', *Art Monthly*, July
Martin Herbert, 'Not Always the Same', *Time Out*, 10–17
September
Sally O'Reilly, 'Not Always the Same', *Art Monthly*, October
2002 Paul Hedge, 'Hard Labour', *Art Review*, December/January
Carlos Navarette, 'Limite y Continuidad', *Disenu*, November
2001 Alex Coles, 'Drawings', *Art Monthly*, May
'Famous for fine art', *Insight*, The London Institute
2000 Deborah Schultz, 'The Office of Misplaced Events (Temporary
Annexe)', *Art Monthly*, February

Louise Coysh, 'New Contemporaries 2000', *AN Magazine*,
August
1998 Sophie Berrebi, 'ne me quitte pas', *Frieze*, January/February

# ACKNOWLEDGEMENTS

Published on the occasion of the exhibition

ANNA BARRIBALL

30 September – 27 November 2011
MK Gallery, Milton Keynes
Exhibition curated by Anthony Spira, with Emma Dean

21 January – 9 April 2012
The Fruitmarket Gallery, Edinburgh
Exhibition curated by Fiona Bradley, with Samantha Woods

Organised by MK Gallery and The Fruitmarket Gallery,
with support from The Henry Moore Foundation,
Frith Street Gallery, the Exhibition Circle of Friends of MK Gallery
and the Commissioning Patrons of The Fruitmarket Gallery
and those who wish to remain anonymous.

Published by The Fruitmarket Gallery, Edinburgh
and MK Gallery, Milton Keynes

Publication supported by Frith Street Gallery
17–18 Golden Square, London, W1F 9JJ
Tel: +44 (0)20 7494 1550, Fax: +44 (0)20 7287 3733
info@frithstreetgallery.com, www.frithstreetgallery.com

Edited by Fiona Bradley
Designed and typeset by Elizabeth McLean
Assisted by Susan Gladwin

Photographers: Gautier Deblonde, Galleri Bo Bjerggaard,
Copenhagen, Daisy Hutchison, Hyjdla Kosaniuk, J. Littkemann,
Dave Morgan, Jonathan Shaw, Pete White, FXP Photography,
Steve White, Woodley and Quick Photography

Distributed by Art Data
12 Bell Industrial Estate, 50 Cunnington Street, London, W4 5HB
Tel: +44 (0)20 8747 1061
www.artdata.co.uk

Printed by Stewarts of Edinburgh. Printed in the UK

ISBN 978-1-908612-01-4

The artist thanks:
Anthony Spira, Emma Dean, Lee Farmer, Matthew Cross,
Adam Darby, Aaron Head, Tomas Rogers, Katharine Sorenson,
Cleo Walker, Emma Wilde, Luke Williams, Simon Wright and
MK Gallery. Fiona Bradley, Elizabeth McLean, Jamie Mitchell,
Samantha Woods, and The Fruitmarket Gallery. Jane Hamlyn,
Susanna Beaumont, Dale McFarland, Toby Kress, Sophie Scopes
and Frith Street Gallery, London. Bo Bjerggaard, Britt Bjerggaard,
Morten Korsgaard, Bolette Skibild and Galleri Bo Bjerggaard,
Copenhagen. Richard Ingleby, Florence Ingleby, Daniel Smernicki
and Ingleby Gallery, Edinburgh. Michael Dyer Associates,
Bob Pain at Omni Colour, Keith Andrews and Colin Boyse
at Pendragon Frames.

Patricia Chi, Briony Fer, Laura Lord, Lucy McLeod, Greg McLeod,
Annabel Pettigrew, Charlotte Schepke, Mark Titchner,
Mark Wallinger, Richard Woods.

cover: *Shutters* (detail), 2011, diptych, pencil on paper

**MK Gallery**      The Fruitmarket **Gallery**     Frith Street Gallery     The Henry Moore Foundation

THE FRUITMARKET GALLERY

45 Market Street, Edinburgh, EH1 1DF
Tel:+44 (0)131 225 2383, Fax: +44 (0)131 220 3130
info@fruitmarket.co.uk, www.fruitmarket.co.uk

The Fruitmarket Gallery is a publicly-funded art gallery of national
and international significance, and is Scotland's leading
contemporary art space. The Gallery aims to make contemporary
art accessible without compromising art or underestimating
audiences. Its programme of exhibitions of Scottish and
international artists is world-class and always free.

Publishing is an intrinsic part of The Fruitmarket Gallery's creative
programme, with books published to accompany each exhibition.
Books are conceived as part of the exhibition-making process,
extending the reach and life of each exhibition and offering artists
and curators a second space in which to present their work.

The Fruitmarket Gallery is a company limited by guarantee,
registered in Scotland No. 87888 and registered as
a Scottish Charity No. SC 005576 VAT No. 398 2504 21
Registered Office: 45 Market St., Edinburgh, EH1 1DF

The Fruitmarket Gallery staff:
Director, Fiona Bradley
Deputy Director, Elizabeth McLean
Development Manager, Armida Taylor

Research and Interpretation Manager, Stacy Boldrick; Publishing
Assistant, Susan Gladwin; Senior Installation Technician,
Colin MacFarlane; Gallery Manager, Jamie Mitchell; Commercial
Opportunities Manager, Iain Morrison; Education and Outreach
Manager, Caitlin Page; Installation Technician, Simon Shaw;
Finance Manager, Celeste Stamenkovic; Press and Marketing
Manager, Louise Warmington; Bookshop Manager,
Matthew Williams; Administrator, Kirsten Wilson;
Exhibitions Organiser, Samantha Woods

MK GALLERY

900 Midsummer Boulevard, Central Milton Keynes, MK9 3QA
Tel: +44 (0)1908 676 900, Fax: +44 (0)1908 558 308
info@mkgallery.org, www.mkgallery.org

MK Gallery is a purpose-built public gallery in Milton Keynes
presenting changing exhibitions of international contemporary art.
The Gallery provides free access to high quality, innovative and
thought-provoking contemporary art from around the world,
building relationships between artists and audiences.

MK Gallery gratefully acknowledges annual revenue support
from Arts Council England and Milton Keynes Council.

Registered Charity No. 1059678

Chairman of the Trustees: Will Cousins

Trustees: Keith Baker, Peter Butler, Helen Flach, Peter Geary,
John Hawthorn, Simon Ingram, John Lewis, Jacky Scott,
John Skelton, Jill Stansfield

MK Gallery staff:
Director, Anthony Spira

Gallery Manager, Melanie Appleby; Curator of Online Content,
Matthew Cross; Head of Exhibitions, Emma Dean; Head of Learning,
Emma Fry; Informal Learning Manager, Victoria Mayes; PA to the
Director and Events Coordinator, Emily Nixon; Head of
Administration, Fennah Podschies; Communications Director,
Katharine Sorensen; Financial Controller, Lorraine Stone;
Front of House Coordinator, Tara Williamson; Front of House
and Events Manager, Simon Wright; Gallery Assistants: Veda
Beeharry, Veronica Cocca, Henrietta Cooney, Dobrochna Futro,
Hannah Gaunt, Jonny Hill, Sarah Kay, Dawn Law, Masuma Miah,
Clare Ridgeway, Sue Swain

CREATIVE SCOTLAND

ARTS COUNCIL ENGLAND     Supported by     MILTON KEYNES COUNCIL